Darwin's Breath

PRAISE FOR *DARWIN'S BREATH*

In Connie Green's masterful new collection, her poems achieve an amazing task, placing one's own life relics into the billions of years of design by the creative force of the universe. Although the three sections of the book are different, they merge through the power of landscape, family, seasons and a girl growing up in Appalachia, soon learning of a woman's work. The sections join earth's complex existence in *Darwin's Breath* to Green's own personal life evolution. Throughout the book, her poems blossom with painterly, lyrical, sensory passages, enough to fill a treasure chest. Connie Green's adoration of those who left beliefs shaped by depression, war, work and the marvel of the natural world creates a transformative effect, teaching the reader an important truth, that in a contemporary society where new means better, we must celebrate frugality, labor and sharing as sacred acts. She quotes Maxine Kumin at the beginning of "Parsimonious," "Saving is a form of worship." No matter the age of the reader, these poems will bring her home again, to a heritage of sacrifice for the common good, which we must continue to celebrate, treasure "until only moonlight / and the whisper of an owl's / wing measure out the rhythm/of our grateful hearts."

—Bill Brown

The poems in Connie Jordan Green's collection, *Darwin's Breath*, remind me of the wisdom found in the work of Mary Oliver and Wendell Berry, which understands that looking clearly at the world and offering an accurate rendering of its natural processes remains the poet's truest calling. Green offers extremely well-made poems about making, suffused with the pleasures of craft and quality work. In *Darwin's Breath*, poems of science and poems of the spirit hold their own beside one another without contradiction. Both modes of understanding the world reflect the wonder we might feel at spiders coaxing their webs through thin air, or at the cosmos contained in one small rock, and turning through it all, "Memory like / a Ferris Wheel," as in the poem "This Do in Remembrance." Connie Jordan Green's poems invite the reader to inhabit them, and to share in their quest for the fullness of life.

—Jesse Graves

Darwin's Breath

Poems

Connie Jordan Green

Iris Press
Oak Ridge, Tennessee

—

Cover Photograph: Guilherme Stecanella

Book Design: Robert B. Cumming, Jr.

Iris Press
www.irisbooks.com

Library of Congress Cataloging-in-Publication Data

Names: Green, Connie Jordan, author.
Title: Darwin's breath : poems / Connie Jordan Green.
Description: Oak Ridge, Tennessee : Iris Press, [2018]
Identifiers: LCCN 2017059618 | ISBN 9781604542462 (softcover : acid-free paper)
Classification: LCC PS3557.R3635 A6 2018 | DDC 811/.54—dc23 LC record available at https://lccn.loc.gov/2017059618

Acknowledgments

Grateful acknowledgment is made to the editors of the following journals and anthologies in which the poems listed were published the first time, sometimes in a slightly different form:

2nd & Church, 2012: "Growing Up Female"

Anthology of Appalachian Writers, Vol.vii: "Darwin's Breath," "Love Poem at Seventy-five"

Anthology of Appalachian Writers, Vol. viii: "Tiny House," "Singing," "The Swan"

Anthology of Appalachian Writers, Vol.ix: "Attic Room in January"

The Avocet: A Journal of Nature Poetry, Fall 2017: "Approaching October," "A Red-Tailed Hawk" (reprinted)

The Avocet, Weekly: "Last Snow?" (forthcoming)

The Avocet, Weekly #239: "Around the Garden, Early Evening"

Connecticut River Review, 2014: "City Moment"

Cumberland River Review, Fall 2015: "Turning the Corner"

drafthorse, 2015: "Elegy for a Farmhouse," "In November," "In the Art Gallery," "Newcomers," "Want"

Fluent, Spring 2014: "Paradise"

Jimson Weed, Spring 2016: "Grief," "A Red-Tailed Hawk," "Vining"

The Notebook, The Grassroots Women Project, Fall 2013 : "Language"

The Notebook, The Grassroots Women Project, Spring 2014: "Squatters"

The Notebook, The Grassroots Women Project, Winter 2016: "Earth Her Abode," "Preserving"

Now & Then, 1999: "Home"

Pine Mountain Sand & Gravel, Vol. 18: "Peeling Potatoes"

Pine Mountain Sand & Gravel, Vol. 20 (forthcoming): "Woman Leaving"

Poem, May 2003: "First Frost"

Potomac Review, Spring 2016: "Iris"

Sow's Ear Poetry Review, Winter 2015: "Vigil"

Sow's Ear Poetry Review, Winter 2017: "Reading Neruda on a September Afternoon"

STILL: The Journal, Summer 2016: "Ode to the Apple"

STILL: The Journal, Winter 2017: "The Color of Comfort"

Third Wednesday, Spring 2015: "June Prayer," "Welcome Summer"

Wavelength, #8: "The Ballet Class Tea Party"

Whale Road Review, Spring 2017: "Remnant"

I am indebted to those who have taught and inspired me, those who have critiqued and cajoled the poems into their public shape, and those who have been my companions in the effort to get a little writing done whenever possible. In particular, I want to thank my writing group, the East Tennessee Writers; the November Retreat Women; Phyllis Price for helping order the poems; the line of poets who have led thirty-years' worth of workshops for Tennessee Mountain Writers, Inc.; Bill Brown for his workshops at Learning Events; Studio Retreat at Lincoln Memorial University for providing a block of time during which to write; all the participants in my classes and workshops who have taught me far more than I've taught them; Bob and Beto Cumming for their long-standing faith in my work. Above all, I am grateful for my husband Dick, our children and grandchildren, and my sisters—all of whom figure largely in everything I write.

—Connie Jordan Green

Family: A group of like things; class.

Contents

III. THE NEWS WE HEAR

I. Darwin's Breath

Evolve: To develop gradually; to work out, devise.

Darwin's Breath

What tone
then for the always ongoing
eavesdrop on our souls?
—Jeff Hardin

When the sun sinks
behind the Cumberland Plateau,
fireflies rise like stars,
and here, perched in the valley,
I think about navigation—
how there are only narrow
ways out, how mountains
loom to the north and west,
spires in the Smokies pierce
the heavens east and south.

My geologist friend tells me
these are the oldest mountains
on earth, tectonic plates
that slipped, slid, elevated,
fossils of deep sea embedded
in ridges, her practiced eye plucking
them from clear cuts, outcroppings:
trilobite, cephalopod, ammonite.

We are made of fragments—
amoeba into fish into amphibian
and mammal, the path
of our development the history
of the world. How then to speak
of the soul, wish for its whisper
as we skirt the ordinary,
waking, sleeping, waking,
our lives deepening into dust?

One Hundred Billion

Is it possible—earth
   composed of the brittle
      broken bones of a hundred
         billion dead who once trod

this ground, who hunted
   the savannahs, settled into
      grain-growing tribes,
         inhabited mesa and river

valley, dwelt upon mountain
   tops, their lives a shadow
      cast at noon by the hawk's
         wild spiral, a cry echoing

where waterfall meets
   deep pool, and trout jump
      at dragonfly, where minnows
         shimmer in the shallows?

Ode to a Small Rock Gathered
on a Fiftieth Anniversary Trip to Maine

You are your own cosmos, molecules
locked together since time began, igneous
messenger from the Mesozoic, from wooly
mammoth and frozen earth, sweep of glaciers.
Neither feather nor bone, yet you tell
of what once lived, molten and flowing.

On summer evenings, moored to a table
where my husband and I watch the sun
drop behind the Cumberland Mountains,
you anchor the newspaper against breezes,
secure the words the way you once
steadied the cliffs against the roar of sea.

By day you witness the beagles returning
from their morning run, the cats curled
atop the porch rail, evidence that cells
once in motion have life forever,
testimony to our fifty-year union,
concrete as granite, enduring as rocks.

Lichen and Seashell

Where dry winds blow
and the rock warms,
where leaf mold
cushions our feet—
this is the place
the lichen grow,
clutching the roughness
of oak bark, clinging
to the side of a stone—
here the hush of day
slides into night—
and beyond the ridges,
past the mountains
and plains dotted with pine,
out where wild currents
beat at the sand, the endless
waves roll and roll, here
the shells—whelk
and crab, swirls and points,
here beige into mauve,
the work of eons accreting,
more eons wearing away,
shell that will one day
return to grains of sand.

Remnant

Here is a butterfly wing,
a scrap like the fabric of a rainbow,

more delicate than a baby's
scalp, this wing caught

on the tip of the pasture grass.
Here is color come to join

the green of the field.

Wind lifts the wing like a sigh,
gentles it to a bed

of stems and leaves where
it will settle like sunlight,

will fade and blend,
and another day will whisper

of all that comes and goes.

Rattlesnake Skin

Not coiled, but curled—
once he was immense,
   a six-foot terror,
      his rattle a warning:
         I mean no harm, stay away.

Once he sunned
on rocky cliffs,
   fed on rats and small rabbits,
      swallowed whole
         the eggs that came his way.

When God thought of wisdom
He envisioned the snake,
   set him to wind
      along the earth, gave
         him a jaw hinged larger

than nightmares.
Now this skin, like fine lace
   our grandmothers tatted,
      is brittle to the touch, holds
         to itself its planes and patterns,

will not yield its secrets,
leaves to our imagination
   the snake's silent slide
      across a dry terrain,
         how earth blessed his passing.

A Red-Tailed Hawk

circles and calls, his scolding
a clear yeep-yeep intersecting afternoon's
silence, though silence is a fleeting thing.

When the hawk's ascension reduces
him to a speck against the blue,
jays and mockingbirds resume harassing
the cats on the prowl, my husband and me
as we go about our chores, the world

that never quite conforms to their grumpy
demands. They could be old men propped
on the porch, whittling knives curling
splinters of aromatic cedar while they grumble
about politics and their arthritic joints.

The crows take up their own cawing
over the fields, though the object
of their ire is less obvious, the owl
asleep in his nest, the corn fields
sere and rattling in the September sun.

The planet spins toward equinox,
dark gaining on us day by day,
the hawk watching as earth fades.

The Spider

I dreamed a spider last night,
his legs long, elegant,
his body a melody—black,
brown, high notes of yellow.

Around us the disarray
of humans—newspapers,
cardboard boxes, a plastic bag
filled with dried rose petals.

He strolled up my finger, he
crossed my palm, rested on
my forearm—*far enough*, I said
and gently blew him back.

Memory hunkered beside
him there—tarantula,
black widow, brown recluse, childhood
warnings, spider that once

bit my finger, sharp sting like
a briar when I reach for
the blackest berry, spider I
rescued from my friend's shoe,

tipped into the boxwood, summer's
song around us, last night's
dream spider floating away, his
trapeze a gossamer thread.

Attic Room in January

Beyond the window
blue-green needles
of the spruce,
and a ridge of mountain
against metal-gray sky,
backbone of a slumbering beast
that once bent and bucked,
rose and buckled,
embedded sea shells
where now hawks soar.

In my attic office
I heft words,
hone and polish
them as they settle
against a yellow pad,
graphite glinting
in the morning sun,
an aging woman,
head bowed
to the work she loves.

Iris

Quaker Lady, the garden book names
this shade—pale lavender verging
on the beige of spring oaks, color

seeping petal to petal, frizz of beard
like fluff of cattails too long in the sear
of sun. I have come to cut stems

for my mother, her brain cells
like the iris rhizomes, tangled and twisted,
their flowering a stubborn stand born

of black earth and granite will, of flex
and force, sap spiraling into blade,
spines erect this spring morning

while earth lurches from equinox
to solstice, and Quaker Ladies mass
among mossy stones of an old wall.

Today, the Rain

sheets the window pane,
blurs the mountain ridge
to the west, and I am left

with memory's images—
the farm in our early days,
a cow calling her young,

our own children tucked
each night in their sweet
smelling pajamas beneath

the low eaves, the constellations
hovering beyond the roof top,
joy and her shadow, sorrow,

waiting on our back porch,
the sure way morning
rose in the east, our labor

carrying us through each day,
the years a train we never
realized we had boarded,

the long whistle at each crossing
a summons to what we would
know only in memory, how

each mile became a prayer,
each breath an act of worship.

Vigil

Walk out while the moon rises,
shimmering like satin,

the air wild with change
and the fervor of autumn,

thick with the first hickory
fire and the promise of rain.

You are yourself wild for
change, the last of summer's

heat, the slowly opening door
to winter, the way the moon

charges the landscape. Tell her
you are here, you have been present

while she was away, you wait,
though she vanishes again and again.

The Invisible Realm

I awake to an ordinary
day when the angel of all
that has gone before hovers
like a mist above my bed

and though my husband sleeps
nearby I am in my aloneness
the way a silvery fish drifts with
currents, sequesters the shadows.

No darkness, even the corners
of the room alive with light, my heart
stripped of the demons that chased
me down the long corridors of night

and I think this could be the day
the scarlet tanager spreads her wings
on the lip of the bird bath, the day
a neighbor drops by with a basket

of just-picked beans, this could be
the day I remember my mother
before her Alzheimer's, her voice
lifting in song, the day the ghosts

of my small children play in the grass,
call to one another while twilight seeps
from the valley floor. This is the day
where I belong with a fierceness

that burns like the stars
hurling their flames
through the vacuum of space,
through the vortex of the finite.

The Swan

for Steve Holt

No collection of poems
should be without a swan
on a pond, graceful arch
of neck, orange feet
floating beneath the surface,
black eye and bright beak
a crayon mark against
all that white, the breeze
lifting small waves
while the swan sails
her majestic ship
over the water, the far
shore no destination
but a metaphor
for all that waits.

The Dog Critiques Poetry

No rhetoric to separate metaphor from the way dew
dampens your coat or a creek filled with fish soothes
a summer day, only images lined through the hours—
a hoard of hard, full teats, puppy bodies huddled for warmth,
sticks and balls cushioned in your mouth, a full feeding bowl,
gentle hands roaming head to flank, a stove in winter, earth cool
beneath your belly in summer, rhyme and meter beating
steady as the strokes of geese winging their vee overhead.

A string of sound not unlike barks and growls,
the slow rumble of too much thought, not enough
sniffing after a wild rabbit in the brush. Though
here and there a frenzied yowling over a fox's scent,
a knowledge of ridges giving way to valley where
an open field beckons the long stretch of the race.

Olivia

She is tortoiseshell—orange and black
in a pattern set by a higher power.

She climbs the maple, walks out a limb,
and drops onto the roof, queen of all

she surveys—the distant hills, her sister
below stalking a silvery rodent.

From the porch roof Olivia peers
in my office window, my attic refuge

a part of her daily prowl. If I ignore her,
she'll lie at the point of the roof, dangle

her paws off the edge, doze until the sun
warms her dark fur. She knows climb

and descend, knows laze and pursue,
knows the sound of food pattering

in her bowl, the way the wind will wash
over her when she poses in the open window.

Among the Unseen

So much of the world exists
without us ...
—Gregory Djanikian

dens of rabbits tunneling
beneath the pasture, their presence
detected by the beagle's nose

    the spread of maple roots surrounding
    the house, a maze whose density
    approaches a laurel hell or a brambled hillside

birds that inhabit the wooded acres,
their song insistent in the morning
air, drifting still at sunset

    and so much we hold in our hearts—
    the way a brown field greens
    overnight when March becomes April

the way rain soaks the roots
of corn, funneled by leaf and stalk,
the way day slips into evening

    and night spreads like a moth
    settling her soft wings.

Symbiosis

I want the smell of hay curing
in a June field, the press of wind
against my face, the touch
of a child's hand on my arm.

Day rises beyond the mountains
and I search for what is not there—
my father's back bent to pick beans,
my mother singing over a hot iron.
I am neither he nor she, my own
mingling of cells, magic of birth

when spirit infuses ectoplasm, when
what was not becomes new fire against
the dark. This morning a mockingbird
defends her nest, dives at the cat and will
not leave her alone, her scold as distinctive
as Darwin's finch beak, her bones shaped

through eons, branching away from cardinal,
from jay, her own mockingbird cells rising
on the wind, swooping again and again,
the cat equally evolved into huntress,
and I the face at the window, watching.

This Do in Remembrance

I was hanging clothes,
breeze whipping the sheets
so they wrapped my body
like a shroud, and the sky
was the blue of October,
color of God, winter's chill
as remote as a movie we
once saw, its terror visiting
our sleep until time wore
down its strangeness.

It was a day for the living
though the old friend who
had seen me through our
children's scraped knees,
bruised feelings, through
their spells of running away
or fighting in school
hallways, now lay hooked
to tubes, her brain slowly
filling with blood.

Memory turns
like a Ferris Wheel,
sights glimpsed, gone,
our stomachs rising
like hope in a hospital corridor,
though we know the down swing,
how the familiar will whip
out of sight, how our bodies
come keyed with a code
that spells our names when stars
call back the elements deposited
in the mind of God.

Kin to Planets

On this November morning, boxwood branches
  glisten beneath dew-hung spider webs,
the valley lies white under a blanket of fog,
  and maple leaves drift like an early snowfall.

We are made mutable, bendable as a willow,
  made of stars flung like grains of sand,
capricious as this November day when stillness
  will give sway to swirling wind and lowery sky,

our lives leaning toward the infinite,
  our finite centers yearning toward galaxies.

By the Window

By the window
I prop
my morning cup—
tea simmers
to a dark stain,
steam eddies
around my face.
Sunlight radiates
from the field
and lilac spreads
over the mountain
like a cloth unfurled.

Let morning
sing her song,
let birds rise
on gray wings,
dog enjoy his romp,
cat her prowl,
the day's turning
smooth as a river stone,
the coming darkness
a distant murmur
through willowy
tree tops, a dare
the stout pines reject.

The Color of Comfort

here at the edge / of the abyss
the tea is the amber color / of comfort
—Linda Pastan

and the wind rises
like the breath
of a hundred souls
who have drifted
from the ledge
and settled in the valley
where clover covers
the fields and ivy
climbs the cliff face,
where white-faced
cattle wade waist
deep in summer's
shades of green,
and the stream
that carved the valley
offers a soft murmur
as if it had no power
to wield.

Late

Even this late the bones of the body shine
and tomorrow's dust flares into breath.
—Mark Strand, "The Coming of Light"

You walk out
and the stars
scatter light like dust
from creation's first breath,
and the small thoughts
that all day have sat
on your shoulder
and whispered
their solemn secrets
into your ear
spin off like seeds
from the moon face
of a dandelion.
You know it is only
the coming of night,
the velvet cape
that calms and quietens,
but even this late your bones
sing their old song,
your blood dances to a rhythm
the stars themselves remember.

Ode to the Apple

When you enter the delicate
    presence of the apple

you fall into the shine, through red,
    yellow, wandering among pale shades—

and the tree, the dappled tree
    of white and pink blooms,

cedar waxwings lined on a limb,
    petals beak to beak down the line—

and the first bite of apple
    like starburst on the tongue,

like seawater and salt
    and the freshest peas spilled

from the pod, and when
    apples fill a basket, when

ripe aroma rises from the pan
    and cinnamon and brown sugar

bubble into winter's delicacy,
    when our bodies become the apples

gathered through our sweat,
    when starlight and moonlight

are sentinels seeing us safely
    on our way, and the apple waits—

oh delicate one, oh journey worthy
    of a thousand years, we embrace you.

II.   GRAPEVINE WOMAN

Grow: To develop and reach maturity; thrive.

Grapevine Woman

Like grapevines grown on a southern hillside,
she absorbed minerals: iron a red trace deepening
her blood, zinc in its glinty capsules like mica—
soaked up sun and rain, her limbs sturdy
as hundred-year-old concord stock.

       She was sapphire, topaz, tasted of chardonnay,
       merlot, the acidic pinot noir of a long ferment.

Unpruned, untethered, she stretched over fields,
branched into oak and maple, climbed
where jays, ravens cawed for her sweet fruit.

September Again

When sunlight slips below the eaves
into the kitchen corner,

when blackbirds gather in the oak
and the tree sets up a clatter,

how perfect it all is—
this effort to shed regret

for what has come and gone
and will not come again.

Night hides the dogwood tingeing
red, the cornstalks drying.

No moon to light the fields, to shout *harvest*,
only the last crickets to sing us to sleep.

Reading Neruda on a September Morning

He would have fixed upon the basket of apples, old
Pippins waiting to be made into pie, green skin blemished
by mountain storms, ancestry reaching to a great-great-
grandfather's farm and the rolling hills of his neighbors,
apples Neruda united with full woman and hot moon,
flour and honey in a love sonnet. The cat rubs her back
against my feet, and I hear Neruda extolling the only creature
made perfect, *born completely finished*. I want, and my list
goes on—the esoteric state of happiness, solid comfort
of a cup of tea, sweet breath of another hour. The cat
wants simply the chase, blue-tailed skink across
the deck planks, mouse behind the furnace, swish of cat's
tail a whisper of warning, her single nod to otherness.

Fall Folly

At first she thinks
    black garbage bags,
      torn open and
        drying on the hay bales—

but no, it's crows
    with outstretched wings
      sunning on a
        September afternoon.

Approaching October

Open the window and listen
to the mowing machine clack
through summer's late grass,
to the quiet of birds scooping
insects in their waves of flight.

When I was young I believed
in the dying of the year, in the dry
leaves of the oak, the tall ironweed,
the profligate goldenrod, believed
cold hovered somewhere north
and we were sliding into it.

I am old now, my soul smoothed
by the circling of the years, seasons
softened one into another, pliant
as dough my mother pinched into rolls
that rose like mushrooms after rain.

Open the window and listen
as the wind shifts earth's axis,
tilts us once more away from the sun.

First Frost

Knee-deep in brown vines,
you call *grab the other end*,
tug at the soaker hose,
a black snake twined
in the ruined garden.
Yellow leaves rattle farewell,
no sorrow for green gone,
the lost aroma of tasseling
that thrust bees into ecstasy,
for days of sun,
crows a worshipful chorus.

We'll have the place orderly,
we vow, as we loosen the stiffened
hose, coil and tie it into a ring
to hang like a wreath on the potting
shed wall. Forty winters we've tended
this spot, summer a dream
we almost forget as we blanket
leaves atop frozen furrows.
Behind us the house waits,
windows shut tight, cordwood ricked
and ready, bed a tumble of comfort
for polar nights. Crows worry their way
across the lawn, each hunched step
a curse on the weather. All winter
they'll ride the tops of pines, black
specks scrawling a message on gray skies.
Cold, they'll cry in hoarse voices,
a word we whisper as we work.

Turning the Corner

It approaches in black boots,
stomps the zinnias, lays
bare the garden—tomatoes
limp on spent stems, peppers
dark with loss. Night comes
early, the sun a lazy arc,
her face white with cold.

The red of Virginia Creeper
fades, drops to the littered
ground, leaves a lattice
of bare limbs against the shed
wall. Deck chairs huddle
like summer people abandoned
by their hosts, left to rain and snow.

Sleet will shine the windows,
polish the streets to the sheen
of old tables rubbed by love,
worn by elbows. Hands cradle
cups of tea while wind knifes
through every crack. *Hurry,
hurry*, something says
and we do—hasten all the day
but we cannot outrun it.

Cleaning Off the Garden in Fall

Though my father has been gone
forty-six years, his hands pull
the last squash plants, uproot
cornstalks, pile them into the cart
and wheel them to the horse pasture.

He has inhabited my garden
since late February when I planted
the first row of peas, knelt with me
to tuck broccoli and cabbage sprouts
into earth, oversaw the digging
of trenches for potato eyes, walked
the rows in mid-summer searching
for beetles, the wayward slug, stooped
with me over beans, pulled slender pods
for pot and freezer, tested corn silks
for crispness, a sign of mature kernels.

Now I want neatness of composted
bean plants, only gourds left
to climb the fence, stems drying
in October's slanting sun, all
that was once green departed into earth.
The world leans toward November,
the month of his death, and I am bent
on bareness, dark soil gone to rest.

In November

A rare balmy day in November,
earth dampened by yesterday's
rain, soil ready for digging—
all afternoon I plant daffodils,
small Téte-a-tétes at the front
of the bed, Yellow Trumpets
at each end, and in the center
mixed bulbs to spread
the blooming season
over months of spring.
Clods crumble in my hands,
plugs of earth lift, then
fall again over the bulbs,
all afternoon on my knees,
weather waiting in the west,
sun and labor joined one
last time before the darkness.

Want

We strip green tomatoes
    from withered vines, pluck
        half-grown peppers, call

for a basket, the crop
    more than we'd hoped,
        last yield of summer's abundance,

the gathering a ritual we perform
    year after year as cold creeps
        from the north, encases leaf,

stem, root in a relentless embrace.
    By morning the garden will stand
        stark, black with frost-burn.

We split open peppers, roast them
    in the oven, feast on the tangy
        goodness of their sweet lobes.

Week by week, tomatoes lined
    along the kitchen counter slowly pink,
        an urge toward ripeness unstopped by loss of vine,

our hunger blooming
    stout as winter wind,
        fierce as a wolf's howl.

We Make a Woodpile

It is more wood
than one can imagine—
an oak, long-standing
near the barnyard entrance
trunk's girth
beyond our circling arms.

A chain saw
buzzes its width
sawdust collects
on coats and pants
drifts like snow
beside the downed tree.

Enough wood to build
a small house—
one door, one window
place of warmth and beauty
to keep at bay snow, wind
the cold we banish

as all winter
we carry splintery
split red oak logs
fragrant as fall
to feed
our hungry woodstove.

January Lament

All morning cardinals visit
the feeder, their bright plumage
a remnant of holiday spirit,
a flip of the tail at January's gloom.
Beyond the hill a neighbor spears
a hay bale to the front of his tractor,
chugs the load to cows bunched
in the hollow bellowing their hunger.

In the mailbox, bills pile up
like omens of an approaching
blizzard, and we huddle by the fire,
throw on last summer's apple
prunings, pray for a break
in the weather, though like outcasts
marooned on an island,
we know the worst awaits us yet.

We will not be rescued until days
slide into weeks and months, a river
of time that will wash us up on spring's
shore, scourged and made whole by deprivation.

Last Snow?

Flakes like puffs of down
   fill the bird feeder, upholster
      deck chairs in soft white,
         blanket boxwood and pasture,
            a bed of emerging daffodils.

If this is winter's last fling
   let her play, let her spread
      her arms, engulf us
         in an exuberant beauty
            that silences the highway's

constant song, stills the night
   until only moonlight
      and the whisper of an owl's
         wing measure out the rhythm
            of our grateful hearts.

Going Out

Take with you creek waters
   running clear over mottled
      and mossed rocks, last fall's

leaves like Moroccan leather
   against speckled stones,
      the smell of mint rising.

Take the earthy feel
   of a late-winter pathway,
      the loam you tread mined

by earthworms. Go where robins
   and rufus-sided towhees
      scratch and scavenge,

where gray limbs etch their grace
   against spring's first blue sky,
      where red tints the maple-studded

ridges, and day approaches
   on pussy-willow feet, her neck
      arched for your gentle touch.

Along the Gutter

after Mary Oliver

Along the gutter
something
that is not a limb,
not a mass of leaves

unless leaves
are translucent,
elongated with eyeholes
and a hinged jaw.

This once was
the black snake,
secure in his new body,
shedding the old skin,

on his way into summer,
rodents and the young
of many species
his chosen dinner,

on his way as he
has been for eons,
slither and slink,
sure as a new season.

Welcome Summer

Happiness engulfs me:
    pots of red geraniums on the deck,
        rows of beans heavy with slender pods,
            gourd vines curling along the fence,

    hummingbird at the feeder,
        bluebird at the bath, sky like a bowl,
           white clouds a godly graffiti.

And if contentment
    spills from my pockets, piles up
        like petals around my feet, it is only
           the season, sunlight stretching her limbs

    over the long day, splashing her blessing
        on tree and shrub, lawn and meadow,
           on cow and horse and child and parent,

    all who step out, look around and soak
        up summer like a dry pond enfolded
           at last in the embrace of monsoons.

June Prayer

Let daisies blanket the pasture,
the wren huddle safely
in her house at the eave,
let lady beetles devour
their weight in aphids—
the devil's due swallowed in one gulp—
let lake glint
like metal in afternoon sun,
the moon rise like a spotlight,
cicadas saw their summer song
until June seeps
through our veins
slow as honey, earth's
sweet nectar on our tongues.

Around the Garden, Early Evening

Lovely is the word that comes to mind, though
no one can see loveliness, only its embodiment—

cleome sprout and bloom among the bean
plants, a honeybee sips from the pink flowers,

a row of okra breaks through leaf mulch
my grandson and I spread, a huddle of corn,

tassels beginning to brown, perfumes
the air, the soil a dark depository

of a life's worth of decayed vegetation,
horse and cow manure, the residue

of chicken litter from those years
my daughter raised her feathered flock—

the fence walling in the garden, weathered
and wobbly, holding deer at bay, its gate waiting.

Serving Beans to the Family

Dear children, this is not purgatory.
Let us consider the lowly bean,
basic food through the ages.

When man stopped roaming the savannah, spear
in hand, and settled down, he perfected the bean—
grown from early legume into legends of length
and beauty, its slender body food for palates
more refined with each generation—sautéed, boiled,
roasted, eaten raw, stirred with onions or tomatoes,
seasoned with salt pork or vinegar and sugar.

Beans raised in backyards, bunched or climbing,
picked by the bushel, broken, tossed into a pot.
Beans that provide blossoms for bees, offer their
leaves to fuzzy beetles, caterpillars. Beans my father
grew in long rows, back-breaking to the child
with a hoe, the picker with his basket. Beans
that gift the soil with their nitrogen-fixing habit.

Beans that you will eat, my children, fresh
off the vine, and all winter frozen beans
to restore summer, bring us again to days
in the sun, gathered around our dinner table.

Small Consolations

The way clematis
    climbs the garden
        fence

sunflower stalks
    sprout in sidewalk
        cracks

maple seedlings
    spring up in
        any bare spot

and Virginia creeper
    gallops over
        the aged potting shed—

summer smells
    of honeysuckle,
        privet hedge in flower

my husband's hands
    stroking the dog's
        ears, plucking ticks.

Summer Quilt

a river where bamboo
creeps along the banks,
poles for my dad's beans

those bamboo sprouts,
sticks my sisters and I
ride into evening

a campfire dying
at lake's edge,
trotlines hidden

all that is red
and orange glowing
on a summer afternoon

the smell of rain
after a long
drought

the bowl of constellations
emptying over
our heads

fireflies flowering
in the trees
on June evenings

the way children
disappear down the driveway,
their voices less than bird cries

The River

This is the road of ancient times.
This is the silent path.

Cattails lift their fat cigars.
Red-winged blackbirds flash rainbows.

Beware the muddy bank, silt deep
as quicksand, black as veins of coal.

Here is the current, swift and dark.
Here the sycamore leaf floats face down.

In the shallows hatch of mosquito eggs,
squiggles of larvae a watery constellation.

Somewhere a fish, scales of silver,
eyes of isinglass, glides on the pebbly bottom.

Come to the river when sunlight
pierces the arching shade.

Come when rain pricks your skin.
Come when gnats hang heavy in the air.

Here is the river, ancient road.
Here is the secret path.

Late August

Dog days and humidity,
too much sun and too much
of all we longed for. Weather
plunders our carefully tended
garden where we dedicated
the holiness of labor, absolved
our bodies of winter's sins
of glut and languor. Now
we stand in sun's slanting
rays, blink in the dwindling
light, willing to forfeit the pleasure
of sweat, the soreness of muscles,
only the bean beetles left to trip
among the wilted stems, to hollow
the last life liquid from each leaf.

Vining

Gourds grow along the garden fence,
vines cover wooden planks, fruit
droops, yellow and green and warty.

I think how like old age, even
the bugs tunneling their way
into the hearts of the gourds—

until I round the corner where clematis
climbs the same fence, spreads
along the top rail, summer seasoning

tight buds that, come fall, will burst
into a haze of white blossom, scent
the hillside, sweet as all last things.

Thinking of Walt Whitman

Love the earth and sun and the animals.
—Walt Whitman

Yes, even when the temperature hovers week
after week in the nineties, humidity encases you
like a blanket—love the earth for the first blue
morning glory blooming on the garden fence,
the field of Queen Anne's lace bobbing in afternoon
waves of heat. Love the sun that urges buds into fruit,
the nib of squash behind the fertilized bloom into long,
green zucchini, more and more each time you look.

Love the animals that prowl the garden
while you sleep—raccoons in the corn, possums
in the compost, long slender snakes that threaten
bird nests and mice alike, owls that call their
distant mates, hawks that all day spiral into
the dome of haze and heat that holds you close.

III. The News We Hear

Nourish: To provide with food and other substances necessary for life and growth; feed.

What She Wants

Beneath a sign saying "free,"
an array of hardbacks,
their orderly spines
jacketed in multi-colors.
She takes two, tucks them
into her market basket
with a bag of lettuce,
a loaf of bread,
a bundle of bay leaves.

At home she slices the bread,
tears off a chunk of lettuce,
lets the bay bask in the windowsill's
sun. She adds the books
to the army marching
along her shelves.

What she wants
stacks up beside them—
a weedless garden, soft light
by her reading chair, a silky
body in bed beside her yearning limbs.

At night the house pops
and sighs, its stories locked tight,
wanting out, the siding weathered
through an avalanche of years.

The Dance

Dirt decorates the front yard, swept dirt,
its care the dance she and the broom execute—
one, two, three, step and twirl—the evenings
of her early life trip through her mind,
young men waiting to whirl her around
the dance floor, the future a jazz band, woodwinds
and brasses in syncopation—and now the broom,
only the broom, her children nap across
her bed, her husband deep in the mines,
she and the broom waltz across the dark
earth, a symmetry of strokes in their wake.

Parsimonious

Saving is a form of worship.
—Maxine Kumin, "The Path, the Chair"

Children of Depression-era
parents, schooled in thrift,
we worshipped bits of foil
we rolled into ever-growing
balls, donated at last to the war
effort. Adults, we chose life
on a farm where leftover
baling twine ties up tomato
plants, soil from the mushroom
factory feeds their roots,
where a leftover house sprouts
new rooms on three sides,
weather-tight windows, solid
floors, where a worn-out mower
harbors parts for its replacement—
gaskets and gears, spark plugs,
magneto, carburetor, wheels
and frame, where day by day
we piece a life grown holy
with the rub and shine of use.

Paradise

after Arthur Smith

I used to live in a similar place. At noon
the sun poured over the mountain,
spread her molten heat like the hottest
ember in the coal grate. By evening
the hollows steamed, cooled overnight
by a draft from deep mine shafts,
by breezes sweeping down the hillsides.
Summers were eternal, winters like
a plunge into ice water, spring
broke in a rapture of bloodroot,
hepatica, trailing arbutus, chartreuse
trees shimmering on the ridges, autumn
like an artist gone mad with his brushes.

I used to live where cousins were daily
companions, where my grandfather's
hot toddy started the day, my grandmother's
black skillet was always frying up chicken,
where my father wore coal dust and my
mother sang, sang, sang the day away,
used to live in a house small as a shoe
box where Christmas and Easter created
happy chaos, where childhood diseases
sulfured the air, and always the windows
gleamed, the porch boards were nailed
tight, and love cupped her hands
around us all, lived there in my child-
hood disguise, filling, filling the vessel
of self, honey to last a lifetime.

Growing Up Female

My husband remembers wars
he and his friends fought—
two or three boys holed up
in a shack, he and Henry outside,
BB guns finding holes and cracks
in the walls, emptying their weapons
randomly into the openings. And later,
wild rides with under-aged drivers
in their fathers' borrowed cars,
tires squealing on Dead Man's Curve.
He climbed cliffs and dared buzzards,
declares one lifted him with its huge
talons, set him down in a grassy field,
safe for one more war.

Courageous, my sisters and I crossed
the turnpike behind our house,
waded the creek where run-off
from a battery shop rainbowed
the surface, returned home
to tie sleeves of chenille
bathrobes around our waists, twirl
on our toes, rose-colored fabric
swirling around us, barefoot ballerinas
whose lives flowed on a swell of music.
War intruded only as flickering newsreel
at Saturday's matinee, our minds rejecting
the images, nimble as Ginger Rogers
dancing backward across the screen.

Language

for my sister

Those afternoons we walked home from school,
damp leaves beneath our feet stirring mustiness,
remembered smell of our grandmother's root
cellar. You stopped often, rubbed your legs, said
you were tired. We sat on fallen logs, spring
blooming overhead in red maple,
along the hillside in bloodroot, white carpets
as inviting as sheets on our bed.

Next week you were in the hospital—
rheumatic fever, words that meant nothing,
your absence its own vocabulary,
a dictionary I would study month
after month as your heart, that captive flutter
behind your rib cage, taught itself a new language.

Woman Leaving

When the woman leaves the mountains
she carries her childhood in a sling.

She has outgrown weeping
but its wells spring within her.

She bears in her memory
the dead snake around her neck,

the drunken father,
the supper-less evenings.

Above her the ridges are the stern
backbone of her people, they send

a sheltering shadow, a breeze
to stir the ribbon in her hair.

When the woman awakes far
from the mountains, she hears

not the hawk's shrill cry to his mate
but the neighbor's quarrel with his wife.

She steps into a world of factories
and bombs, her life a metaphor

for the blood that rivers its way
through vein, artery, and mountains.

Peeling Potatoes

When we came home from school
she stood by the window, pot
of water on the counter, pile
of potatoes beside her, peels
unfurling like ribbons, exposing
white flesh that would cook
into savory beds for gravy
or fry into crisp mouthfuls.

She pried away spots of rot,
poked out eyes, salvaged all
that was edible. My sisters and I
sat nearby, dipped into milk
the cookies she'd earlier baked,
never thought about the scrubbing,
paring, chopping, boiling, braising,
the daily cleaning, weekly washing,
starching, ironing that filled her life,

one year rolling into another,
the edge of her knife, like stones
in ancient creek beds, worn
to the curve of a potato.

More Than a Thousand Doors Ago

A thousand doors ago,
when I was a lonely kid …
—Anne Sexton, "Young"

We walked the mile to school, government
houses lined the road like a forest
of one species, and in the asphalt-
sided schoolhouse maps hung in cases,
rolled like shades on our bedroom window.

Breezes blew through open windows, doors,
the classroom on May afternoons filled
with the sweet smell of honeysuckle,
mockingbird's scold—our longing for school
to end a line we clung to, hauled ourselves
hand over hand above the murky depths
of China's products, fractions' puzzle—
rote of spelling lists holding us like anchors.

Singing

Through the window, you might think
she's rehearsing for the Sunday choir,
song being the expression of praise,
the exhaling of joy, lungs swelling,
the diaphragm releasing pent-up air,
mouth pursed in vowel and consonant.

But it's only the old favorites
blaring from her kitchen radio,
Patti Page, the Andrew Sisters crooning
their ballads, she joining in to belt out
the tribulations of the day while
her arms swing dishes from dirty pile
to sink, her hands awash in soap suds,
a clean plate its own hymn of praise.

Those Girls

We were the girls with ponytails,
jeans rolled just below our knees,
skates clamped to our tennis shoes,
skate keys hanging from our belts.

We were the girls under the elm,
comic books spread on a quilt,
sunlight through the leaves
like a window opened from heaven.

We were girls of graveled sidewalks,
cars parked against the curb—gray
Frazier Manhattan, black Ford coupe,
crank-down windows and sissy knobs.

We were girls when grass clippings
sprayed from lawn mower reels,
our fathers gripped the wooden
handles, their muscles tight ropes.

Those were our mothers beyond the windows,
looking out over the kitchen sink, dishes
in suds, just out of sight, a pot of beans
on the eye of the stove, steam rising.

Tiny House

This has been / the tiny house
in which we all / have, at one time, lived.
—Laura Kasischke

and loved, and in which
we watched while our parents,
always old, we thought,
became the people we are now,

the house where they cared for us
while we, unknowing, came in
and went out, went out again and again,

where daylight climbed
the east wall, and the moon
lighted our bedtime rituals,

where dogs and cats fed and played
and aged faster than we
who thought we'd always
be young, would always

live in the tiny house,
a pot of potatoes boiling
on the stove, our parents'
heads bent over pages of shuffling

numbers, stretching their work
hours, calculating food and heat,
storms gathering and vanishing

while we spread our paperdolls
over the chenille-covered bed
and pretended lives far away
from the tiny house.

The Ballet Class Tea Party

silks and tulles
       ephemeral
              as a pirouette

bites of melon
       round and fragrant
              as a young girl budding

Woodworking

It was not anything we expected—
our father's woodworking skills
in their infancy, the class
he was taking in the evenings
after a day's work at the government's
gaseous diffusion plant, riding
a bicycle the length of the world's
longest building—his escape into
a world of table saws, jigsaws,
sanders, the piercing aroma
of stain and varnish—and here
beneath the tree on Christmas morning,
a small corner cupboard, pine
boards smoothed and sealed,
doll's dishes aligned on shelves,
here the gift my sisters and I shared
for years, tucked into our bedroom,
a tea-time treat for our make-believe
hours, here the cupboard, storehouse
of memories, a father's first clumsy
cuts and his love placed
where we could not forget.

Pet Graveyard

Mostly we buried goldfish, metallic
scales gone dull as the August sky
behind its valley haze. Bits of asbestos
siding formed the headstone, chips

we shoved into the soil, small patch
of bare earth over which we echoed
the preacher's words—dust to dust—
though there had been nothing

dusty about the fish slipping around
the bowl where we imprisoned our pets,
their fiery color at odds with the green
castle we provided for their entertainment,

house of holes as unnatural as the dirt
where finally they lay, pets we'd never
cuddled or stroked, who knew us only
by the film of food floating overhead.

Girls on the Brink

Young girls flip the pages of magazines,
      imagine breasts they'll wear like jewelry,

the eyes of young men a matching gemstone.
      Their mothers warn them about boys

with tattoos, body piercings, forbid red
      stilettos, fishnet hosiery, walking

alone at night. Young girls gather pieces
      of their lives, horde them in boxes covered

with seashells, grow into prom dresses, wrist
      corsages, bouquets they press dry,

their mothers' lips drawn tight, frowns riding
      the mothers' brows like a ship cresting

the horizon, mothers who once shrugged off
      their own mothers' advice against chewing

gum, boys with ducktails. Young girls want
      what has no name, a longing too large

for the pockets of their tight jeans, too
      flamboyant to fan out in public,

longing that shimmers like oil on water,
      their bodies a shadow in their beds.

City Moment

The girl in the cropped shirt
waits for the bus. Sunlight
glints on metal in ears
and eyebrows, tattoo
along her upper thigh
rises like the sigh
heaving the chest of the old
man standing nearby.

At the end of the block
the bus chugs out a message
of arrival, the girl
hitches back pack to shoulder,
shrugs an arm through the strap
and swings onto the bus,
the old man certain this
bus will take him nowhere,
his desire like diesel fumes
settling along the curb.

1992—To My Mother

It was the year a Democrat
    was elected to the White House,
      a decade of drought
        began in the South,

computers moved
    into every home, cell phone towers
      sprouted like dandelions
        along the Interstate.

It was the year the Methodist
    preacher went off for a rest-cure,
      the Baptist preacher went off
        with the choir director.

It was a year of body piercings,
    sagging jeans, purple hair,
      and glue sniffing. It was the year
        of my second grandchild's birth,

the year the doctor said
    Alzheimer's, your brain cells
      entangling, a maze you would
        wander for seven more years.

What Walks at Night

Just past midnight the nurse heard her cough,
held her hand while the last breath shuddered
through her lips. We lay sleeping, our dreams
crowded with gardening and haying, with
grandchildren who would visit on Sunday.

Listen, dark world, there is more going on
in the ether than conscious mind can know,
more visits of the spirit than daylight allows.

Up the dusty road a stranger limps, walking stick
in one hand, battered hat hiding his face, the wheeze
of his breathing a song we'll learn, the cadence
of his footsteps a dance we'll join, moonlight
silvering our shoulders like fallen stars.

Earth Her Abode

My grandmother, dead forty
years, walks outdoors with me.
The aroma of Southernwood
bordering an old cabin site drifts
on the air, the smell of the chest
where her underthings and lace-
trimmed handkerchiefs nestled.

A pink rose climbs the garden fence,
could have twined over her doorway.
Iris in yellow, blue, mauve are orchids
she wore to church late April and early
May. Lavender's narrow leaves surge
back from winter-killed stalks, pliable
as her hands rolling out biscuit dough.

A rock chimney laced with lichen,
distant mountains dark against pale
blue sky, ladybug crawling along
a grass stem, pebble smoothed
by water and years—nature's quiet
triumphs, fleeting as the draft
on my neck—the wind as she passes by.

Newcomers

That first year we were desperate—
twenty-four cows and an empty barn loft,
early September beckoning with the first tint
of yellow. The farm was worn out, fences sagged,
equipment meant to be drawn by horses.

Cows gazed at us from sere pastures,
their hips like shoulder blades raised
in a resigned shrug. We were twenty-
four, town-bred, toddler in hand,
baby in the womb. Necessity set the pace—

Farmall tractor hitched to clackety mower,
hay laid on the ground, rake next,
pulled field's length, then my husband
down from the tractor, up on the hay rake,
raise the rake teeth, down from the rake,

up on the tractor, turn tractor and rake
to start a new row, down from the tractor,
up on the rake, lower the rake teeth,
down from the rake, up on the tractor,
pull another windrow, at the end of the field

repeat the dance, all day in summer sun,
piling the scant hay into windrows.
Late day, unhitch hay rake, hitch wagon
to tractor. Early evening, pitchfork loose hay
onto wagon, pull the load to the barn,

pitchfork hay into barn loft, the week's
work scarcely a shadow in one corner
of the cavernous space. Next day we sold
all but a few brood cows. They, like us,
hunkered down for the long hunger of winter.

After Waxing the Floors

The cat reclines on a cushion
in a patch of sunlight, smell
of paste wax sweet in the air.
The promise of March hovers
beyond the window.

She is oblivious to my hours
of cleaning and waxing.
She senses some just god
has granted her a warm place.
When she has napped enough

she stretches, yawns, lounges
on the lamp table and enjoys
the show. Birds flit from tree
to feeder, the tip of her tail
twitches, her jaws chatter—

all of life a rhapsody
of small pleasurable minutes.

Home

Nothing matches—
rooms of drywall, rooms of paneling,
vinyl windows, wood windows,
old paneled doors and new hollow-core ones.
I wrap it about me like an afghan
knitted from leftover pieces.

Distant mountains mark life's edge,
a green quilt tucks in the vegetable garden,
color points the flowerbeds like a Cezanne—
remember, Marilyn tells me, he missed his mother's
funeral because the light was right—
sage studs the herb bed, thyme carpets it.

I drink it like my morning cup of tea.
All day it swims within me,
carries me to shore while
lungs and heart swell with longing.

My sister says travel, see the world while you're able.
She cannot know the world lines the study walls,
squirms beneath the garden soil,
lifts its wings over the pasture,
sees its mate spiraling against a summer sky,
and sings, sings, sings.

Learning to Mother

It is best at night,
their bodies snug
beneath sheets,
eyelashes fluttered
to stillness on skin
that seems transparent,
the vinegary smell
of childhood a perfume
you inhale one last time
as you tuck them in,
these children who have
raced through your day,
have ravaged your hours
and filled you with doubt,
their delicate bones
a frame you yearn
to flesh so full
neither stone nor stick
nor storm of your own
rage can ever break.

Grief

When Baxter, old dog of arthritic hips
who came to my daughter in the winter
when she had borne her first child, came
as a bag of bones and mangy fur, ancient
in appearance, the dog the vet assured her
was young, would survive with care,
the dog she nursed along while her son
fed at her breast, Baxter who could not
be contained by chainlink or wooden fence,
who chewed or dug or climbed his way
out of any enclosure to stand in the street
and welcome the neighbors returning from work,
dog who came to live with my husband and me,
who walked the pasture with us, slept with
our resident dogs, ate from their bowls, watered
with them, when he died, at twelve years
of age, the others—Maggie, Hannah, Tilly—
each in turn entered his empty doghouse,
circled and circled again, lay in the doorway,
head on paws, rose, walked out into the sun,
homage to the old dog who once lived among them.

Preserving

All summer I hoe rows of corn, careful
around the roots, the way my father taught me.
I step among squash vines, feet seeking
bare earth, avoid the spread of umbrella-like
leaves, pluck hidden fruits from their private
caves. My harvest basket spills over.

When I bend to the green beans,
I see his back, shoulders scorched
from hours in the sun, bald spot
at the crown of his head peeling.

My mother received his bounty, skinned
and quartered and boiled and canned
so that all winter we ate the goodness
his labor earned, her labor preserved.

Just so my husband and I stand at the kitchen sink,
dunk tomatoes into boiling water, then into cold,
slip skins, chunk the red fruits into quarts to line
our shelves. Gone so soon the years of planting
and growing, my parents' toil meeting our physical
needs: work our heritage, days seemingly endless.

In the Art Gallery

a hacksaw and a swing
blade, each suspended
on two nails against a cream-
colored wall, zip-ties of chartreuse
and fuchsia adorn them
like flags calling the laborer
from toil, work into play—

       no grease and grime, no
       odor of oil or the well-worn
       glow of metallic surfaces
       where my husband's hands
       grip and cajole,
       convince the unbendable
       to give a little,
       conform to the sketch
       his mind continually evolves,
       his labor a recreation
       that fills his being,
       his hands the prayer
       he daily becomes,
       his life its own art gallery.

Love Poem at Seventy-Five

At twenty I could not imagine the slow
aging of the body—hair gray, skin
a thin membrane cradling our bones, spine
slipping to gravity's pull—could not
imagine life stretched across decades,
holding us together through children
and their daily hurts, through the deaths of parents
and friends, through the wild ride of days and nights.

I never imagined the quietness
of a house where two people, twined by
the years, move in unison, how it would
be when lust and longing calmed into joy,
hands touching across a table, snug fit
of bodies side by side fifty-five years.

These Objects

Though sunlight slips between window-blind slats,
you sleep, your tumbled hair, once brown now white
as the sheets, objects of our days mute as we—
your field boots lined beneath the bench, our black
metal bed heaped with quilts against cold our aged
house invites in, dresser where grandchildren's
photos change with each school year, our own
children innocent in frames blooming with dust.

How many things shadow our days, belongings
so familiar we scarcely see them—your father's
hammer hanging from your tool belt, my mother's
rolling pin nestled among can opener, slotted spoons.
Clear as the scrawl on a legal document,
these objects sign our names.

Sunday Morning, Mid-July

We sit on the deck, Sunday paper
spread between us, coffee gone cold.
The distant peal from Woodlawn Baptist
Church calls people to worship.

We are parishioners at the Church
of the Dying Spruce, tree grown
from the sprout our good friends
gave in memory of my father forty-

some years ago, tree now a stilt bearing
a halo of green. The cat creeps to my chair,
climbs to my shoulder and stretches
out, safe from the mockingbird

scolding from the maple. The resident
wrens have fledged a nest, but sit
on another secreted in the hanging
begonia. I envy their second chance,

the opportunity to get parenting right
this time. The breeze picks up, you gather
newspapers, go inside, the house a cave
beneath the trees, a place of hieroglyphics

on the walls, secret messages I've spent
a lifetime deciphering, all around me
the lessons. Beyond our hill, trucks
grind along the highway, the hum

of their passing broken by a siren's
scream, a sound that sets the beagle
baying. I wonder, as I always do,
if the noise hurts his ears or if he hears

in the call the howl of a kindred spirit.
Though it's Sunday, someone is burning
brush, and the smell of wood smoke snakes
up our hill, pulls me back to winter evenings

around the fire, our children, heads bent
over books or board games, waiting
to grow up, wishing themselves into
something they cannot know not to want.

Squatters

I

When we moved to the farm
the barn stood surrounded
by oaks, loft yawning empty
though July was half gone.
More enduring, we thought,
than the land itself— weathered
by wind and blizzard, place
of horses' retreat, their long faces
poking from shuttered openings, eyes intent
upon green pasture stretching to the horizon.

II

Decades later, the barn collapsed
into earth's waiting arms, an end
it had contemplated during rain
and snow, sun and storm,
through generations of horses and cows.

III

Still the '40 Ford pickup grazes
in the vacant lot, paint sloughing
from red to rust, tire rubber crazed
like an ironstone plate, windshield
cracked, one headlight dangling
like a cartoon character's eye
in a barroom fight. She has outlasted
sedans, convertibles, modern minivans,
sports utility vehicles with their tough-guy
attitude. No longer expecting rescue
or revitalization, she has claimed
her patch of land, planted herself
more firmly on earth than animal or building,
her final obedience only to nature's law.

Elegy for a Farmhouse

Old shelter, the men who built
    your frame, cut and sawed, planed
        and nailed, who raised your skeleton—

a cathedral of sweet lumber,
    their sweat a sacrament—
        are long buried in the cemetery

at the foot of the hill. The children
    who dug in the dirt around your
        foundation, who swung from

the nearby oak, fell asleep
    beneath the eaves, lulled by rain
        on your roof, are gone into old age,

stooped and whitened while you
    stand as you have a hundred years.
        You are the way we know

morning: sun rises in the bedroom
    window, crows caw in the field,
        a neighbor's tractor chugs

its work song. You are the day's
    labor—broom and dustcloth,
        skillet and saucepot,

the rhythm of hunger
    and food, of need and plenty.

The News We Hear

The news we hear is full of grief
for that future, but the real news
inside here is there's no news at all.
—Rumi

Monday, like a door opening
into an unknown room, bread rises
on the kitchen counter, a breathy
presence in the quiet.

And Tuesday, sheets flap on the line
while crows caw from hayfields
as if darkness is a part of sunlight,
as if the shadow of a wing passing

overhead is no more than the sound
of trucks jake-braking on the highway.

Wednesday with its news of another
plane downed over another ocean,
and the heart of one more Mideastern
country spilling over its borders,
refugees huddled beneath blankets.

Thursday the tractor breaks down,
Friday the pressure gauge quits
so the water pipes gurgle and
spit out one last drop.

Saturday, the day of all lost things,
a letter slips behind the sofa,
the brooch your grandmother left
you gone from its case,

though by Sunday the morning star
will linger so that you'd swear you
see its imprint on the bedroom door.

PRAISE FOR *DARWIN'S BREATH*

"I think about navigation," Connie Jordan Green writes in the title poem of *Darwin's Breath,* her second full-length collection, "how there are only narrow / ways out." Although the attention of this expansive books stays deceptively close to home, exploring the daily occupations of the poet as she cuts "stems / for my mother, her brain cells / like the iris rhizomes, tangled and twisted" and of the human and other animals that share her place in the Tennessee Valley, it also reaches far out through "stars / hurling their flames / through the vacuum of space, / through the vortex of the finite" and back again through "the years a train we never / realized we had boarded" to visit her young self and to watch as "parents, / always old, we thought, / became the people we are now." Green is a fine poet, and I am happy to follow her expert navigation through the many places these poems go.

—Pauletta Hansel,
Cincinnati Poet Laureate, 2016-2018

Darwin's Breath connects us to those who have come before—Neruda, Oliver, grandmothers, fathers, grapevines, and rocks. It rises "like mushrooms after rain" or "dough my mother pinched into rolls" to illustrate a lifetime of growth. A life, here, measures not in coffee spoons but tea cups, potato parings, spelling lists, and clods of broken earth—over which the gardener kneels knowing that gain is always two parts loss.

—Amy Wright

— Phyllis Price

Connie Jordan Green lives on a farm in Loudon County with her husband Dick, a retired engineer. Her weekly column for the *Loudon County News Herald* is in its 40th year. She writes stories for young people, poetry, and novels (*The War at Home* and *Emmy*, both reissued by Tellico Books, an imprint of Iris Publishing Group, both originally published by Margaret McElderry Books, Macmillan, now Simon Schuster). The novels received various awards: *The War at Home* was placed on the ALA List of Best Books for Young Adults, both books were selected by the New York City Library as Books for the Teen Age, *The War at Home* was nominated to the 1991-92 Volunteer State Book Award Master List, and *Emmy* was selected as a Notable 1992 Children's Trade Book in the Field of Social Studies.

Her poetry has appeared in numerous publications and has won many awards. She has two chapbooks from Finishing Line Press, *Slow Children Playing* and *Regret Comes to Tea*. Her full-length collection, *Household Inventory*, received the Brick Road Poetry Press Award in 2013. She was the recipient of a Lifetime Achievement Award from the East Tennessee Hall of Fame for Writers and was honored by the Arts Council of Oak Ridge. She does volunteer teaching for the Oak Ridge Institute of Continued Learning (ORICL), and frequently leads writing workshops.

CPSIA information can be obtained
at www.ICGtesting.com
Printed in the USA
LVOW03s0452100418
572878LV00001B/41/P